BACK TO ONE!

Your Comprehensive Guide to
Beginning Filmmaking

Written By Greg Galloway

©2024 Greg Galloway

Table of Content

Chapter 1: Introduction to the Art of Filmmaking

- Understanding the allure and importance of filmmaking in contemporary society.
- Exploring the historical evolution of cinema and its impact on culture.
- Defining the roles and responsibilities of key players in the filmmaking process.

Chapter 2: Discovering Your Filmmaking Passion

- Encouraging self-reflection to identify personal motivations and interests in filmmaking.
- Exploring different genres, styles, and themes to find your creative niche.
- Engaging with influential filmmakers and analyzing their work for inspiration.

Chapter 3: Building Your Filmmaking Foundation

- Outlining the essential knowledge and skills required for successful filmmaking.
- Recommending resources for learning about film theory, cinematography, and storytelling techniques.
- Discussing the importance of practice, experimentation, and continuous learning in honing your craft.

Chapter 4: Preparing for Your Filmmaking Journey

- Setting realistic goals and expectations for your filmmaking endeavors.
- Creating a personalized action plan with achievable milestones and deadlines.
- Assembling your filmmaking toolkit, including equipment, software, and resources.

Chapter 5: Crafting Your Cinematic Story

- Exploring the elements of effective storytelling, including plot, character, theme, and structure.
- Providing guidance on developing compelling characters, engaging dialogue, and intriguing plotlines.
- Offering exercises and prompts to help brainstorm and refine your film ideas.

Chapter 6: Planning Your Production Process

- Detailing the various stages of pre-production, including scriptwriting, storyboarding, and casting.
- Discussing the importance of budgeting, scheduling, and logistics in ensuring a smooth production.
- Providing tips for assembling your production team, securing locations, and acquiring necessary permits.

Chapter 7: Lights, Camera, Action: Filming Your Story

- Exploring the fundamentals of cinematography, including framing, composition, and camera movement.
- Offering techniques for directing actors, capturing dynamic performances, and fostering creativity on set.
- Discuss strategies for managing time, resources, and unexpected challenges during production.

Chapter 8: Bringing Your Vision to Life in Post-Production

- Providing an overview of the post-production process, including editing, sound design, and visual effects.
- Introducing popular editing software and techniques for assembling footage, refining pacing, and enhancing storytelling.
- Discussing the importance of collaboration, feedback, and iteration in achieving your artistic vision.

Conclusion: Embracing Your Filmmaking Journey

- Reflecting on the transformative power of filmmaking and the personal growth it fosters.
- Encouraging continued experimentation, exploration, and innovation in your filmmaking practice.
- Providing resources and next steps for furthering your education, networking with industry professionals, and sharing your work with the world.

Before We Begin...

As a young-ish black filmmaker, I am acutely aware of the barriers and challenges that often stand in the way of marginalized voices in the film industry. This structured eBook serves as a beacon of hope and empowerment for aspiring filmmakers like myself, providing a roadmap to navigate the complexities of the filmmaking journey.

From conceptualization to production and post-production, the eBook leaves no stone unturned, offering a comprehensive overview of every step of the process. As someone who has often felt excluded from mainstream narratives, I appreciate the inclusive approach of this resource, which acknowledges the diverse perspectives and experiences of filmmakers from all backgrounds.

What sets this eBook apart is its emphasis on practical advice, creative exercises, and insightful tips. Rather than simply imparting knowledge, it invites readers to actively engage with the material, fostering a sense of agency and ownership over their creative journey. As a black filmmaker, this hands-on approach is particularly valuable, as it empowers me to explore my own unique voice and vision in a medium that has historically marginalized voices like mine.

Through the powerful medium of film, I believe we have the ability to challenge stereotypes, amplify underrepresented voices, and reshape the narratives that shape our collective consciousness. This eBook provides the tools and inspiration to do just that, encouraging readers to harness their passion for storytelling and use it as a force for positive change in the world.

In an industry where black voices and stories are often overlooked or appropriated, this eBook is a testament to the power of representation and diversity. It sends a powerful message to aspiring filmmakers of color that their stories matter, their voices deserve to be heard, and their presence in the industry is not only welcome but essential.

As I embark on my own filmmaking journey, I am grateful for the guidance and support that this eBook provides. It reminds me that no matter the obstacles I may face, my passion for storytelling is a powerful force that can transcend barriers and make a meaningful impact on the world. With its practical advice, creative exercises, and insightful tips, I feel empowered to pursue my dreams with confidence and determination, knowing that my voice has the power to inspire, uplift, and transform.

Chapter 1: Introduction to the Art of Filmmaking

Film is more than just entertainment; it's a powerful medium that shapes culture, inspires change, and captures the essence of the human experience. I have a personal mantra; I make content that educates, entertains, and inspires. In this chapter, we will delve into the captivating world of filmmaking, exploring its significance in contemporary society, tracing its historical evolution, and unraveling the roles and responsibilities of those who bring cinematic visions to life.

Understanding the Allure and Importance of Filmmaking in Contemporary Society

Filmmaking holds a unique allure in contemporary society, captivating audiences across the globe with its ability to transport them to new worlds, evoke deep emotions, and provoke thought. From Hollywood blockbusters to independent films, the art of filmmaking encompasses a diverse range of genres, styles, and narratives that resonate with people from all walks of life.

At its core, filmmaking is a form of storytelling—an art form that transcends language barriers and cultural divides to connect with audiences on a profound level. Through the lens of a camera, filmmakers have the power to explore complex themes, challenge societal norms, and ignite conversations about pressing issues facing humanity.

Moreover, the influence of filmmaking extends beyond the confines of the silver screen, shaping popular culture, influencing fashion trends, and inspiring social movements. Iconic films have the power to leave a lasting impact on society, shaping our perceptions, beliefs, and aspirations for generations to come. I would also say that if you're reading this book, you have a feeling, a fire to create the next global cultural contribution. I think that's what we're all looking for when we lie in bed at night. We all want to make a difference in the world. No better way to do that than the all-encompassing medium of film.

Exploring the Historical Evolution of Cinema and Its Impact on Culture

The history of cinema is a rich tapestry woven with innovation, creativity, and technological advancements. From the Lumière brothers' first public screening of a motion picture in 1895 to the rise of streaming platforms in the digital age, the evolution of cinema has mirrored the social, political, and cultural shifts of the times.

Throughout the 20th century, cinema emerged as a dominant form of mass media, captivating audiences with its ability to entertain, educate, and inspire. From the golden age of Hollywood to the French New Wave movement, filmmakers around the world pushed the boundaries of storytelling, experimenting with new techniques, styles, and narratives.

The impact of cinema on culture cannot be overstated. From influencing fashion trends to shaping political discourse, films have the power to reflect, critique, and reshape society's values, beliefs, and aspirations. Whether through powerful documentaries that shed light on social injustices or timeless classics that capture the human condition, cinema has the ability to leave an indelible mark on the collective consciousness of humanity.

Defining the Roles and Responsibilities of Key Players in the Filmmaking Process

Filmmaking is a collaborative endeavor that requires the collective effort of a diverse team of individuals, each playing a vital role in bringing cinematic visions to life. From the visionary director to the talented actors, cinematographers, and editors, every member of the filmmaking process contributes their unique skills, talents, and expertise to create a cohesive and compelling cinematic experience.

At the helm of the filmmaking process is the director—a visionary storyteller who oversees every aspect of the production, from script development to post-production editing. Working closely with the director is the producer, responsible for securing funding, managing budgets, and ensuring the smooth execution of the project from start to finish.

Additionally, the cast and crew play crucial roles in bringing the director's vision to fruition. Actors breathe life into the characters, infusing them with depth, emotion, and authenticity. Cinematographers capture stunning visuals that transport audiences to new worlds, while editors weave together incongruent elements to create a seamless and immersive viewing experience.

In essence, filmmaking is a collaborative art form that relies on the collective talents and efforts of individuals from diverse backgrounds and disciplines. By working together towards a common goal, filmmakers have the power to create cinematic masterpieces that entertain, enlighten, and inspire audiences around the world.

As we embark on this journey into the world of filmmaking, let us embrace the transformative power of storytelling and celebrate the enduring legacy of cinema as a reflection of the human experience.

Chapter 2: Discovering Your Filmmaking Passion

In the vast and dynamic world of filmmaking, embarking on your journey begins with a crucial step: discovering your passion. Much like a compass guiding a traveler through uncharted territories, understanding what drives you in the realm of filmmaking will serve as the cornerstone of your creative endeavors. This chapter delves into the process of self-reflection, exploration, and analysis necessary to uncover your filmmaking passion.

Encouraging Self-Reflection

At the heart of discovering your filmmaking passion lies the process of self-reflection. This introspective journey involves delving deep into your innermost thoughts, desires, and experiences to uncover what ignites your creative spark. Consider your earliest memories of film - what movies resonated with you on a profound level?

Were there particular scenes that stirred your emotions or characters you deeply connected with? By examining these moments, you can start to identify the themes, genres, or storytelling techniques that captivate your imagination.

Furthermore, reflect on your personal motivations for pursuing filmmaking. Is it the desire to evoke powerful emotions in your audience, to shed light on important social issues, or to escape into fantastical realms of imagination? Understanding your underlying motives will provide clarity and direction as you navigate the diverse landscape of filmmaking. You should also consider your resources, while we want to create the most profound world-changing film, what you need to do first is what anyone who is great at what he or she does; and that is- practice. If you don't learn anything, I hope you take this one thing away from all of your reading, and that is, nothing should stop you from pursuing your dreams. If you come up with a great idea for a film, don't take "no" for an answer, figure out how to bring your idea to life within the parameters of your resources.

Exploring Different Genres, Styles, and Themes

Filmmaking is a kaleidoscope of genres, styles, and themes, each offering its own unique allure and creative possibilities. Take the time to explore a wide range of cinematic expressions, from the visceral intensity of action films to the poignant intimacy of character-driven dramas. Experiment with various storytelling techniques, such as nonlinear narratives, surreal imagery, or documentary realism, to uncover where your creative instincts thrive.

Moreover, immerse yourself in different thematic landscapes, from love and loss to adventure and redemption. Consider how these universal motifs resonate with your own life experiences and worldview. By exploring diverse genres, styles, and themes, you will gradually uncover your creative niche - the intersection where your passions and talents converge to form a distinct filmmaking voice.

Engaging with Influential Filmmakers

In the pursuit of discovering your filmmaking passion, look to the masters who have paved the way before you. Engage with the works of influential filmmakers across different eras and cultures, analyzing their films with a discerning eye. What techniques do they employ to convey their artistic vision? How do they navigate complex themes and emotions with cinematic finesse?

Take inspiration from legends like Stanley Kubrick, whose meticulous attention to detail and visual storytelling revolutionized the medium. Study the bold narrative experimentation of directors like Quentin Tarantino, who fearlessly push the boundaries of conventional storytelling. Delve into the poetic realism of filmmakers like Wong Kar-wai, whose evocative imagery and atmospheric soundscapes transport audiences to ethereal realms of emotion.

By critically engaging with influential filmmakers, you will glean valuable insights into the craft of storytelling and discover new avenues for creative expression. Analyze their films not only for technical prowess but also for the underlying themes, motifs, and character dynamics that resonate with you on a personal level.

Discovering your filmmaking passion is a deeply personal and transformative journey, requiring introspection, exploration, and engagement with the rich tapestry of cinematic artistry. By encouraging self-reflection, exploring diverse genres, styles, and themes, and engaging with influential filmmakers, you will gradually uncover the creative essence that fuels your artistic vision.

Embrace the journey with an open heart and a curious mind, for it is in the process of discovery that true artistic mastery is forged. Remember, your filmmaking passion is a beacon that will guide you through the challenges and triumphs of your creative odyssey, illuminating the path towards realizing your cinematic dreams.

Chapter 3: Building Your Filmmaking Foundation

In the vast landscape of filmmaking, laying a solid foundation is paramount to success. Chapter 3 explores the essential knowledge and skills required to navigate the intricate world of filmmaking, emphasizing the importance of continuous learning, practice, and experimentation in honing your craft.

Essential Knowledge and Skills

Filmmaking is a multifaceted art form that encompasses a wide array of disciplines, from storytelling and cinematography to editing and sound design. To embark on your filmmaking journey, it is essential to acquire a comprehensive understanding of these fundamental elements.

First and foremost, grasp the principles of storytelling - the backbone of every successful film. Learn to craft compelling narratives, develop complex characters, and structure your story for maximum impact. Understand the nuances of plot development, character arcs, and thematic resonance to captivate your audience from start to finish.

Furthermore, familiarize yourself with the technical aspects of filmmaking, including cinematography, lighting, and sound. Master the art of framing, composition, and camera movement to visually convey your narrative vision. Experiment with different lighting setups to create mood and atmosphere, and explore the intricacies of sound design to immerse your audience in the world of your film.

Additionally, develop proficiency in the post-production process, including editing, color grading, and visual effects. Learn to weave together disparate elements into a cohesive whole, manipulating time, space, and emotion to enhance the storytelling experience.

Recommended Resources

Fortunately, a wealth of resources exists to aid aspiring filmmakers in their quest for knowledge and skill development. From books and online courses to workshops and film festivals, there are countless avenues for learning about film theory, cinematography, and storytelling techniques.

Start by delving into the rich tradition of film theory with seminal texts by luminaries such as Sergei Eisenstein, Andre Bazin, and David Bordwell. Explore the principles of mise-en-scène, montage, and genre theory to deepen your understanding of cinematic language and aesthetics.

For hands-on instruction, enroll in online my Filmmaker Academy courses offered very soon on www.2-G4me.com . This and other platforms provide comprehensive training in various aspects of filmmaking, from screenwriting and directing to cinematography and editing.

Additionally, seek out mentorship opportunities with experienced filmmakers in your local community or through online forums and networking events. Learn from their insights, glean wisdom from their experiences, and leverage their guidance to accelerate your growth as a filmmaker.

Importance of Practice and Experimentation

Establishing a solid foundation in filmmaking requires active engagement and continuous learning. It is a journey characterized by hands-on experience, persistent practice, and a willingness to explore new territories within the realm of visual storytelling. By immersing oneself in various aspects of filmmaking, individuals can deepen their understanding, refine their skills, and unleash their creative potential.

Getting behind the camera regularly is not merely about capturing images but about honing one's craftsmanship through practical application. Whether it involves shooting short films, capturing everyday moments, or delving into innovative techniques, each opportunity presents a chance to expand one's repertoire, test ideas, and refine their artistic voice.

Experimentation plays a pivotal role in this growth process. Trying out new approaches, tools, and technologies fosters creativity, flexibility, and adaptability. It encourages filmmakers to push boundaries, break conventions, and discover fresh ways of visually expressing their narratives.

Embracing these opportunities for hands-on experience and experimentation not only enhances technical proficiency but also nurtures a filmmaker's unique style and perspective. It cultivates a mindset of curiosity and exploration, propelling individuals towards new artistic horizons and enabling them to evolve as storytellers.

In essence, by actively embracing every chance to engage with the craft of filmmaking, from the mundane to the extraordinary, aspiring filmmakers can lay a robust foundation that paves the way for growth, innovation, and artistic fulfillment in their cinematic pursuits.

Don't be afraid to make mistakes or fail - it is through these experiences that you will learn and grow as a filmmaker. Take risks, push boundaries, and challenge yourself to think outside the box. Embrace failure as an essential part of the creative process, recognizing that each setback brings you one step closer to mastery.

Moreover, commit to lifelong learning and continuous improvement. Stay abreast of emerging trends and technologies in the industry and remain open to new ideas and perspectives. Attend workshops, seminars, and film festivals to expand your horizons and connect with fellow filmmakers.

In conclusion, building your filmmaking foundation requires a combination of knowledge, skill, and dedication. By acquiring a comprehensive understanding of storytelling, mastering the technical aspects of filmmaking, and embracing a mindset of practice and experimentation, you will lay the groundwork for a successful career in the dynamic world of cinema.

Chapter 4: Preparing for Your Filmmaking Journey

Effective preparation serves as the linchpin for success in the multifaceted realm of filmmaking. In a landscape teeming with creative possibilities and logistical complexities, the meticulous groundwork laid before embarking on a cinematic endeavor can mean the difference between a haphazard effort and a triumphant production.

Chapter 4 encapsulates the vital foundation of planning that underpins a filmmaker's journey. It illuminates the significance of setting realistic goals that act as guiding beacons, steering individuals towards tangible achievements amidst the vast expanse of their cinematic ambitions. By defining clear objectives that are both inspiring and within reach, budding filmmakers can channel their energies purposefully and measure their progress with precision.

Furthermore, the chapter delves into the intricate art of crafting actionable plans, elucidating the transformative power of methodical organization and strategic foresight. Through delineated steps, timelines, and contingency measures, filmmakers can navigate the labyrinthine twists and turns of the creative process with confidence and agility, transcending potential obstacles with poise.

Equally indispensable is the imperative of assembling the requisite tools and resources, a process underscored within Chapter 4's narrative. By procuring not only the tangible equipment but also the intangible skills, knowledge, and networks essential to cinematic craftsmanship, aspiring filmmakers fortify their arsenal for the arduous yet exhilarating odyssey that lies ahead.

Through a tapestry of anecdotal accounts and practical advice, this chapter serves as a beacon of wisdom for those venturing into the luminescent yet daunting world of filmmaking. It bestows upon them the invaluable gift of insight, igniting their creative spirits and equipping them with the acumen to navigate the labyrinthine path with clarity, resilience, and unwavering determination.

Setting Realistic Goals and Expectations

Setting realistic goals in filmmaking is crucial for several reasons. First, it helps filmmakers stay focused on achievable milestones, ensuring progress and motivation throughout the production process. By breaking down the larger vision into smaller, manageable tasks, filmmakers can maintain a clear direction and track their advancements.

Moreover, managing expectations is key to avoiding disappointment and burnout. Recognizing the limitations of resources, budget, and time allows filmmakers to make strategic decisions and adapt creatively within constraints. It also fosters a more positive and collaborative working environment, where everyone involved understands and works towards common, achievable objectives.

While the allure of cinematic greatness can be inspiring, grounding aspirations in practicality and feasibility is what transforms dreams into tangible results. This approach fosters a sense of responsibility and accountability, encouraging filmmakers to develop creative solutions, innovate within boundaries, and realize their vision effectively.

Ultimately, balancing ambition with realism is a delicate but essential art in filmmaking, enabling creators to navigate challenges, seize opportunities, and bring their stories to life with purpose and clarity.

Consider the story of Sarah, a budding filmmaker with grand visions of creating a sweeping epic on a shoestring budget. Eager to make her mark in the industry, Sarah threw herself into the project, pouring countless hours and resources into production. However, as the challenges mounted and the budget stretched thin, she found herself overwhelmed and disillusioned with the process.

Through this experience, Sarah learned the importance of setting achievable goals and tempering her expectations. Rather than attempting to tackle a massive project right out of the gate, she began by focusing on smaller, more manageable endeavors. By setting realistic goals and milestones, Sarah was able to celebrate incremental successes and build momentum over time, laying the foundation for larger projects down the road.

Creating a Personalized Action Plan

This personalized action plan not only outlines what needs to be done but also specifies how, when, and by whom each task will be accomplished. It covers everything from logistics to artistic choices, budgetary constraints to creative freedoms. All of these interconnected components are essential for the success of a cinematic project.

Creating a personalized action plan is a critical step in the preparation phase of any filmmaking project. It demonstrates the filmmaker's foresight, diligence, and passion, and brings their dreams and aspirations to life. The plan serves as a blueprint for turning their vision into a timeless cinematic masterpiece.

To illustrate this, let's take the example of Alex, a filmmaker who wanted to make a documentary about his hometown's music scene. Alex recognized the importance of meticulous planning and created a comprehensive plan that broke down the project into actionable steps with clear milestones and deadlines. From conducting research and securing funding to scheduling interviews and scouting locations, Alex left no stone unturned in his quest to bring his documentary to fruition. By adhering to his carefully crafted action plan, he was able to navigate the complexities of production with confidence and precision, ultimately delivering a compelling and impactful film that resonated with audiences far and wide.

Below you will find a sample of an action plan that will guide you in your endeavor to create your own.

1. **Script**: Write a script that can be filmed on a minimal budget. Focus on simple locations, a small cast, and limited special effects.

2. **Crew**: Keep the crew small but efficient. Look for passionate individuals willing to work for experience, exposure, or a small stipend.

3. **Equipment**: Use affordable or borrowed equipment. Consider smartphones with good cameras, basic lighting kits, and simple audio recording devices.

4. **Locations**: Opt for free or low-cost locations like public parks, schools after hours, or friends' houses. Obtain necessary permits or permissions.

5. **Cast**: Seek volunteer actors from local theater groups, acting classes, or community boards. Look for talented amateurs who are passionate about the project.

6. **Costumes and Props**: Utilize items from the actors' wardrobes and personal belongings. Thrift stores and DIY solutions can also provide cost-effective options.

7. **Shooting Schedule**: Plan a realistic shooting schedule to minimize the number of shooting days. Consider weekends or evenings to accommodate cast and crew availability.

8. **Post-Production**: Edit the film yourself using free or low-cost editing software. Focus on enhancing the story and performances through editing techniques.

9. **Soundtrack**: Use royalty-free music or work with local musicians willing to provide their music for exposure.

10. **Promotion**: Leverage social media platforms to promote the film, create behind-the-scenes content, and engage with potential audiences. Submit to film festivals with low entry fees or free submissions.

11. **Networking**: Connect with other independent filmmakers, attend local film events, and engage with film communities online to gather feedback and potentially collaborate on future projects.

Assembling Your Filmmaking Toolkit

No filmmaker is complete without their toolkit - a comprehensive arsenal of equipment, software, and resources to aid in the creative process. From cameras and lenses to editing software and sound equipment, each tool plays a vital role in bringing your vision to life on the silver screen.

Consider the journey of Michael, a filmmaker who embarked on his first independent feature film with little more than a shoestring budget and a passion for storytelling. Determined to make the most of his limited resources, Michael scoured online forums, attended workshops, and sought advice from seasoned professionals to assemble his filmmaking toolkit.

Armed with a basic DSLR camera, a handful of lenses, and a laptop loaded with editing software, Michael set out to capture his vision on film. Despite facing numerous challenges along the way, from equipment malfunctions to unforeseen logistical hurdles, he persevered, leveraging his creativity and resourcefulness to overcome each obstacle in his path.

Through his journey, Michael learned that while state of the art equipment can certainly enhance the filmmaking process, it's ultimately the filmmaker's ingenuity and passion that drive the project forward. By assembling a toolkit tailored to his specific needs and budget constraints, he was able to channel his creative energy into a compelling and authentic cinematic experience.

If you're in need on guidance for what this toolkit should consist of, you should take note of the tool kit I use in each production.

1. **Smartphone or Entry-Level Camera**: Use a smartphone with a good camera or an entry-level DSLR

camera for filming. I wouldn't spend money on a prosumer camera for your first production. You will need that money for other aspects of production including a small contingency amount for when things don't go as planned. As long as your camera can shoot 4k, you'll be in good shape. On several of my films, I've used a Cannon M-50 and it has worked wonders and earned over eighty thousand in revenue.

2. **Tripod**: Invest in a sturdy tripod for stable shots, panning, and tilting.

3. **External Microphone**: Purchase a lavalier microphone or shotgun microphone for better audio quality.

4. **Basic Lighting Kit**: Acquire affordable LED lights or DIY lighting solutions to improve the lighting quality of your scenes. I use GVM, Neewer, and Small Rig lights; they're affordable and they rival any of their more expensive counterparts.

5. **Reflector**: Use a collapsible reflector to bounce and diffuse natural light for better lighting control. Reflectors are used for outdoor lighting when there is a good amount of daylight available. When you don't have a power source, sometimes a reflector that bounces the daylight from the sun onto your subject will do the trick.

6. **Props and Costumes**: Gather a small collection of props and basic costumes that fit the needs of your script. In an ultra-low budget production, you would do better to ensure your story takes place over short time span so you won't need a lot of wardrobe changes. In addition, ask your cast to provide their own wardrobe. You can also make a prop list and circulate it amongst your cast and crew to keep your props budget down as well.

7. **Scriptwriting Software:** Use free scriptwriting software like Celtx or an open-source alternative for scripting.

8. **Non-Linear Editing Software**: Utilize free or low-cost video editing software like DaVinci Resolve, HitFilm Express, or Lightworks for post-production. For

9. **Release Forms**: Prepare basic release forms for actors, crew members, and location owners.

10. **Location Scouting Checklist**: Develop a checklist for location scouting to find suitable, low-cost, or free filming locations.

11. **Storyboard Templates**: Utilize free storyboard templates or software to plan out your shots effectively.

12. **Call Sheet Template**: Create a template for call sheets to organize shoot schedules and inform crew and cast about daily activities. I use the production and scheduling features in Celtx, I generate all of my schedules including call sheets from the app. Once you breakdown your script in the software (I provide a tutorial of script breakdowns in my online academy) it will be easy to generate schedules and reports.

13. **Soundproofing Materials**: Consider using blankets, pillows, or sound foam to improve audio quality in makeshift recording spaces. This is a requirement when recording ADR for you film in a home studio, but if you can find an inexpensive recording studio then that will save you time.

14. **Music and Sound Effects Library**: Access royalty-free music and sound effects libraries for post-production audio needs. Having a subscription to Motion Array, Soundstripe, Artlist.io, Epidemic Sound, Premium Beat are great options for adding sound to your film or trailer, but if you don't have the budget for such a subscription, try out Bensound.com, incomptech.com, or freemusicarchive.org for music you can use under the creative commons rules.

15. **Online Distribution Platforms**: Research cost-effective online distribution platforms for sharing and promoting your finished film. As you know YouTube, Vimeo, and Amazon Video Direct or options for self-distribution and Tubi is an option through an aggregator

or distribution company (although I highly discourage using a distribution company) to release your films. You can also sign up for a Content Provider account on my new streaming platform stayconnectedtv.com for an easy to use, filmmaker friendly platform to monetize your content. If you'd like to sign up for an account, go to: stayconnectedservices.com/filmmakers to get started.

16. **Social Media Scheduler**: Use free social media scheduling tools to plan promotional posts and engage with your audience effectively.

Preparing for your filmmaking journey requires a delicate balance of ambition and pragmatism. By setting realistic goals, creating actionable plans, and assembling the necessary tools, you can chart a course toward success in the dynamic and ever-evolving world of cinema. Remember, every filmmaker's journey is unique, but with dedication, perseverance, and a dash of creativity, the possibilities are limitless.

Chapter 5: Crafting Your Cinematic Story

In the realm of filmmaking, the heart of any great film lies in its story. Chapter 5 delves into the art and craft of crafting cinematic narratives, exploring the essential elements of effective storytelling, providing guidance on character development, dialogue, and plotlines, and offering exercises to help hone your film ideas. Through anecdotal accounts and practical advice, this chapter serves as a roadmap for aspiring filmmakers as they embark on the journey of crafting their cinematic masterpieces.

Exploring the Elements of Effective Storytelling

At its core, effective storytelling is about more than just recounting events; it's about captivating your audience, evoking emotion, and leaving a lasting impression. To achieve this, filmmakers must master the fundamental elements of storytelling, including plot, character, theme, and structure.

Consider the journey of Emily, a filmmaker with a passion for storytelling. Inspired by classic films like "Casablanca" and "Citizen Kane," Emily embarked on a quest to understand the secrets of great storytelling. Through extensive study and experimentation, she discovered the importance of crafting a compelling plot that keeps audiences on the edge of their seats, rich and nuanced characters that resonate on a deep emotional level, and themes that explore the human condition in all its complexity.

Armed with this knowledge, Emily set out to bring her own stories to life on the screen, weaving together intricate narratives that captivated and moved audiences in equal measure. Through her journey, she learned that while the elements of effective storytelling may vary from film to film, the underlying principles remain constant: engage your audience, stir their emotions, and leave them with something to ponder long after the credits roll.

Guidance on Character Development, Dialogue, and Plotlines

Characters are the beating heart of any captivating narrative, serving as the lifeblood that infuses depth, emotion, and meaning into the story's tapestry. Be they virtuous heroes or malevolent villains, resilient protagonists or cunning antagonists, characters function as the vital conduits through which audiences immerse themselves in the vicissitudes of the story's universe.

In the realm of filmmaking, the art of character development stands as a cornerstone of crafting a cinematic opus that resonates with viewers long after the credits roll. Rich in nuance and imbued with complexity, well-crafted characters transcend the confines of mere plot devices, emerging as sentient beings with aspirations, flaws, and evocative histories that mirror the kaleidoscope of human experience.

These characters imbued with multidimensionality and emotional resonance, serve as the narrative's guiding lights, propelling the story forward through the tempestuous currents of conflict, growth, and revelation. Each character, whether a paragon of virtue or a harbinger of chaos, contributes a unique hue to the vibrant canvas of the cinematic narrative, enriching the tapestry of human emotion and experience that unfolds before the audience's eyes.

By delving deep into the intricacies of character development, filmmakers unlock the power to forge a visceral connection between the audience and the on-screen denizens, fostering empathy, intrigue, and investment in their journeys. As viewers witness the trials, triumphs, and transformations of these characters, they are afforded a glimpse into the intricacies of the human condition, evoking laughter, tears, introspection, and catharsis in equal measure.

In sum, the cultivation of rich and multidimensional characters lies at the crux of sculpting a cinematic magnum opus that lingers in the hearts and minds of audiences long after the projector dims. Through the alchemy of character development, filmmakers summon forth a pantheon of figures whose indelible presence infuses the story with vitality, authenticity, and enduring resonance, crafting a memorable and immersive cinematic experience that transcends the boundaries of time and space.

Take, for example, the case of David, a filmmaker who struggled with creating believable and relatable characters for his films. Frustrated by his lack of progress, David sought guidance from mentors and fellow filmmakers, who encouraged him to delve deeper into his characters' motivations, fears, and desires.

Through this process of introspection and exploration, David discovered the importance of crafting characters with depth and complexity, each with their own unique quirks, flaws, and inner conflicts. Armed with this newfound understanding, he set about breathing life into his characters, infusing them with authenticity and humanity that resonated with audiences on a profound level.

Dialogue and plotlines are essential pillars that uphold the edifice of effective storytelling, supplementing compelling characters to construct narratives that resonate deeply with audiences. Through the artful interplay of engaging dialogue and intriguing plotlines, filmmakers imbue their stories with vibrancy, depth, and emotional resonance, weaving a tapestry of imagination and intrigue that captivates viewers from start to finish.

Dialogue, akin to the lifeblood of characters, serves as the dynamic vessel through which thoughts, emotions, and motivations are breathed into existence. When crafted with precision and authenticity, dialogue transcends mere words, evolving into a symphony of voices that reverberate with the cadence of human expression. It not only elucidates the innermost workings of characters but also serves as a conduit through which relationships are forged, conflicts are navigated, and revelations are unfurled, fostering a profound connection between the audience and the unfolding narrative.

Simultaneously, plotlines emerge as the architectural blueprint that delineates the narrative arc, mapping out the ebbs and flows, peaks and valleys that define the trajectory of the story. Like a compass guiding travelers through uncharted terrain, plotlines provide a cohesive structure around which the dramatic action unfolds, steering the audience through a labyrinth of twists and turns towards a climactic and gratifying denouement. They introduce elements of suspense, conflict, and resolution, cultivating a sense of anticipation that compels viewers to remain ensnared within the narrative web until its final revelation.

In essence, the synergy between engaging dialogue and intriguing plotlines forms the cornerstone of effective storytelling, enriching the storytelling tapestry with layers of complexity, nuance, and emotional depth. As filmmakers deftly intertwine these elements, they carve out a narrative landscape that sparkles with authenticity, vitality, and resonance, inviting audiences to embark on a transformative journey through the enchanted realms of human experience.

Exercises and Prompts for Brainstorming and Refinement

Crafting a cinematic story is a deeply personal and iterative process, requiring experimentation, exploration, and refinement. To help jumpstart your creativity and refine your film ideas, consider the following exercises and prompts:

1. **Character Profiles**: Create detailed profiles for your main characters, including their backstory, personality traits, and goals. Explore how their past experiences shape their present actions and motivations.

2. **Dialogue Workshops**: Practice writing dialogue by engaging in workshops or exercises that challenge you to

convey emotion, subtext, and character dynamics through conversation.

3. **Storyboarding**: Visualize your story through storyboard sketches or visual aids, mapping out key scenes and sequences to help visualize the flow of your narrative.

4. **Theme Exploration**: Reflect on the underlying themes of your story, considering how they resonate with your own experiences and worldview. Explore different interpretations and perspectives to deepen the thematic resonance of your film.

Through these exercises and prompts, you can unlock new creative insights, refine your storytelling skills, and bring your cinematic vision to life with clarity and purpose.

Crafting a cinematic story is a labor of love, requiring dedication, passion, and a willingness to embrace the creative process. By exploring the elements of effective storytelling, developing compelling characters, dialogue, and plotlines, and engaging in exercises to brainstorm and refine your film ideas, you can unlock the transformative power of storytelling and create cinematic experiences that resonate with audiences for generations to come.

Chapter 6: Planning Your Production Process

The journey from script to screen is a meticulously planned and executed process, requiring careful consideration of every detail. Chapter 6 delves into the intricacies of planning your production process, detailing the stages of pre-production, discussing the importance of budgeting, scheduling, and logistics, and providing tips for assembling your production team, securing locations, and acquiring necessary permits. Through anecdotal accounts and practical advice, this chapter serves as a comprehensive guide for filmmakers as they prepare to bring their cinematic visions to life.

Detailing the Stages of Pre-Production

Pre-production is the foundation upon which a successful film is built, encompassing a series of crucial stages that lay the groundwork for production. Among the key components of pre-production are scriptwriting, storyboarding, and casting.

Consider the journey of Mark, a filmmaker with a passion for storytelling. Inspired by a vivid dream, Mark set out to transform his vision into a screenplay, meticulously crafting each scene, dialogue, and character arc with care and precision. With the script in hand, he embarked on the next stage of pre-production: storyboarding.

Storyboards serve as visual blueprints for the film, allowing filmmakers to map out each shot and sequence in advance. Armed with a pen and paper, Mark translated his script into a series of detailed sketches, capturing the mood, composition, and camera angles for each scene. Through this process, he gained clarity and perspective on the visual language of his film, laying the groundwork for a seamless production process.

With the script finalized and storyboards in place, Mark turned his attention to casting. Casting the right actors is essential to bringing your characters to life and imbuing your story with authenticity and depth. Through auditions, callbacks, and chemistry reads, Mark carefully selected a talented ensemble cast that embodied the spirit of his characters and brought his story to life with nuance and emotion.

Discussing the Importance of Budgeting, Scheduling, and Logistics

While creativity fuels the filmmaking process, it is tempered by the practical realities of budgeting, scheduling, and logistics. Without careful planning and foresight, even the most ambitious projects can quickly unravel.

Take, for example, the experience of Laura, a filmmaker tasked with producing a low-budget indie film. Faced with limited resources and tight deadlines, Laura knew that meticulous budgeting and scheduling were essential to the success of her project.

Drawing on her background in finance, Laura developed a detailed budget that accounted for every aspect of production, from equipment rental and location fees to catering and transportation. By carefully allocating resources and prioritizing essential expenses, she was able to stretch her budget to its fullest potential, maximizing production value without compromising quality.

In addition to budgeting, scheduling is a critical aspect of pre-production, ensuring that every aspect of the production process unfolds smoothly and efficiently. Through careful coordination and communication, Laura developed a shooting schedule that optimized time, resources, and manpower, minimizing downtime and maximizing productivity on set.

Logistics, meanwhile, encompass a wide range of considerations, from securing locations and acquiring permits to arranging accommodations and coordinating transportation. Through meticulous planning and attention to detail, Laura navigated the logistical challenges of production with ease, ensuring that every aspect of the filmmaking process proceeded without a hitch.

Tips for Assembling Your Production Team, Securing Locations, and Acquiring Necessary Permits

A successful film is the result of collaborative effort, requiring a diverse team of talented individuals working together toward a common goal. Assembling the right production team is therefore essential to the success of your project, encompassing roles such as producers, directors, cinematographers, and production designers.

Consider the example of James, a filmmaker tasked with producing a short film for a prestigious film festival. Recognizing the importance of assembling a skilled and dedicated team, James reached out to his network of collaborators and colleagues, handpicking individuals whose expertise and passion complemented his own.

From the director's vision to the cinematographer's eye for composition, each member of the production team brought a unique perspective and skill set to the table, enriching the creative process and elevating the quality of the final product. Through open communication, mutual respect, and a shared commitment to excellence, James and his team forged a strong bond that carried them through the challenges and triumphs of production.

Securing locations is another crucial aspect of pre-production, requiring careful research, negotiation, and coordination. Whether filming on location or in a studio, finding the right setting for your story can make all the difference in capturing the mood and atmosphere of your film.

For Emily, a filmmaker tasked with shooting a period drama set in 19th-century England, securing authentic and visually stunning locations was paramount to the success of her project. Through tireless research and outreach, Emily scoured the countryside for historic estates, picturesque villages, and grand manor houses that evoked the elegance and opulence of the Victorian era.

Acquiring necessary permits is equally important, ensuring that your production complies with local regulations and ordinances. Whether filming in a public park, city street, or private property, obtaining permits demonstrates respect for the community and helps avoid potential legal issues down the line.

Through careful planning, negotiation, and communication, Emily secured the necessary permits for her locations, allowing her to focus on bringing her cinematic vision to life without the fear of interruption or delay.

Planning your production process is a multifaceted endeavor that requires careful consideration of every detail, from scriptwriting and storyboarding to budgeting, scheduling, and logistics. By detailing the stages of pre-production, discussing the importance of budgeting, scheduling, and logistics, and providing tips for assembling your production team, securing locations, and acquiring necessary permits, this chapter serves as a comprehensive guide for filmmakers as they prepare to bring their cinematic visions to life. Through careful planning, collaboration, and dedication, you can lay the groundwork for a successful and memorable filmmaking experience that resonates with audiences far and wide.

Chapter 7: Lights, Camera, Action: Filming Your Story

As the sun sets behind the horizon and the lights flicker on the set, the moment arrives when the script comes to life, and the cameras start rolling. Chapter 7 is a voyage into the heart of filmmaking - the exhilarating production phase. From the intricacies of cinematography to the nuances of directing actors and managing unforeseen obstacles, this chapter stands as a guiding beacon for filmmakers navigating the thrilling journey of bringing their stories to life on screen.

Exploring the Fundamentals of Cinematography

Cinematography is the soul of visual storytelling, weaving together framing, composition, camera movement, and lighting to create a tapestry of emotions that resonate with audiences. It is the art of capturing images that not only convey the story but also immerse viewers in the world of the film.

Cinematography is instrumental in visually narrating the story, providing a language of imagery that communicates emotions, themes, and messages to the audience. Through lighting, framing, and camera movement, cinematography sets the tone, mood, and atmosphere of a film, influencing how viewers perceive and engage with the narrative. Cinematography can reflect the internal states of characters through visual cues, such as framing choices, camera angles, and proximity to characters, enhancing the audience's understanding of the characters' relationships and personalities.

Cinematography has the power to convey symbolic meanings and themes through visual metaphors, adding depth and complexity to the story beyond the dialogue and plot. By using visual elements, cinematography can underscore and emphasize the central themes of a film, reinforcing the underlying messages and motifs in a subtle yet impactful manner.

The visual aspects of cinematography, such as colors, lighting, and composition, can evoke emotional responses from viewers, enhancing the immersive experience and forging a deeper connection with the narrative. Cinematography aids in guiding the viewer through the narrative, directing attention to key plot points, transitions, and character developments, ensuring a cohesive and engaging storytelling experience.

Cinematography contributes to the overall visual style and aesthetics of a film, shaping its look and feel, and distinguishing it as a unique and artistically crafted piece of work. Through techniques like camera movements, framing, and pacing, cinematography can build suspense, tension, and anticipation, heightening the drama and impact of critical moments in the story.

Effective cinematography can transport the audience into the world of the film, immersing them in the characters' experiences, locations, and emotions, creating a fully engaging and transformative viewing experience.

Offering Techniques for Directing Actors

Central to the success of any film is the performances that bring its characters to life. As the conductor of this symphony of emotions, the director plays a pivotal role in guiding and inspiring actors to deliver authentic and compelling performances.

1. **Foster a Collaborative Environment**: Encourage open communication and teamwork on set, cultivating a supportive atmosphere where the cast and crew feel valued and empowered to contribute creatively.

2. **Empower Actors:** Provide constructive feedback and guidance to actors, allowing them the space to explore their characters' depths and motivations while respecting their creative input and individual interpretations.

3. **Cultivate Creativity and Experimentation**: Embrace a culture of innovation and experimentation, encouraging actors to take risks, improvise, and explore different approaches to their performances to discover authentic and compelling portrayals.

4. **Provide Clear Vision and Guidance**: Communicate your artistic vision clearly to the cast and crew, offering guidance on character motivations, emotional beats, and overall storytelling objectives to ensure a cohesive and coherent production.

5. **Support and Encourage**: Offer support, encouragement, and reassurance to actors throughout the filming process, creating a safe space for them to take artistic risks, make mistakes, and grow, ultimately leading to performances that resonate with audiences on a deep and emotional level.

Discussing Strategies for Managing Time, Resources, and Unexpected Challenges

Production is a battlefield of creativity and logistics, where filmmakers must navigate a labyrinth of time constraints, budget limitations, and unforeseen obstacles. From the chaos of inclement weather to the unpredictability of equipment malfunctions, the ability to adapt and problem-solve is paramount. Sticking to these guidelines will help you manage your production.

Managing an ultra-low-budget film shoot requires careful planning, resourcefulness, and strategic decision-making to maximize limited resources while achieving a high-quality product. Here are detailed instructions on how to effectively manage an ultra-low-budget film shoot:

1. **Script and Pre-Production:** When initiating an ultra-low-budget film project, it is vital to begin with a succinct script that limits the requirement for costly locations,

intricate special effects, and elaborate setups. Prioritizing a compact cast of characters and a restrained selection of locations can significantly mitigate logistical complexities and financial burdens.

Additionally, comprehensive pre-production preparation is essential, encompassing the creation of shot lists, storyboards, and a meticulously crafted schedule to enhance shooting efficiency and streamline the overall production process. This strategic approach lays the groundwork for a successful film shoot within stringent budget limitations, emphasizing resourceful planning and prudent decision-making to maximize the project's creative potential.

2. **Resource Management:** To effectively manage the challenges of an ultra-low-budget film shoot, it is crucial to capitalize on existing resources and locations to minimize expenses. This can involve leveraging friends' houses, public spaces, or accessible props and costumes to avoid costly rentals. Additionally, consider cost-effective approaches like borrowing or renting

equipment at discounted rates or utilizing smartphones for filming if the quality aligns with the project's requirements.

Another valuable strategy is to collaborate with local film schools, community theaters, or organizations to enlist volunteer crew members or cast who are eager to contribute their expertise and time in exchange for valuable experience or industry credit. By harnessing these resourceful tactics, filmmakers can navigate the constraints of a tight budget while maximizing creative opportunities and production value.

3. **Crew and Cast:** In order to optimize efficiency and minimize costs, it is advisable to maintain a lean and efficient crew during the shoot. This involves prioritizing roles that are deemed essential for the production process. Additionally, it is beneficial to select crew members who possess versatility and are willing to undertake multiple responsibilities. This not only streamlines operations but also maximizes productivity.

Furthermore, when considering casting options, it can be advantageous to explore local talent pools. Local actors may be more inclined to work for deferred payment or even volunteer their services in exchange for the opportunity to enhance their portfolios. This approach not only helps to reduce expenses but also fosters community involvement and support within the filmmaking endeavor.

4. **Locations and Permits**: To minimize expenses and streamline the filming process, consider opting for public locations or spaces that do not entail costly permits or location fees. It's crucial to maintain transparency with property owners regarding the project's low-budget nature, seeking their permission to shoot without incurring additional expenses.

Additionally, ensure all necessary permits for shooting in public areas are obtained beforehand to prevent any potential legal complications or disruptions during filming. By taking these proactive steps, you can effectively navigate the logistics of location scouting while adhering to budgetary constraints.

5. **Equipment and Technology**: When managing the budget for equipment and post-production, it's essential to prioritize the acquisition of fundamental tools such as cameras, sound recording devices, and basic lighting setups. These elements form the backbone of any film production and are crucial for capturing high-quality footage and sound. In post-production, consider exploring affordable or free editing software options to effectively manage costs without compromising on quality.

Moreover, to enhance visual aesthetics while keeping expenses in check, maximize the utilization of natural lighting or opt for inexpensive lighting alternatives. By strategically allocating resources and making prudent choices in equipment selection and post-production software, you can ensure the production maintains a high standard of quality while adhering to budget constraints.

6. **Scheduling and Efficiency**: Crafting a well-thought-out shooting schedule is a cornerstone of successful filmmaking, requiring careful consideration of various factors to ensure smooth operations on set. By meticulously planning each day's activities, filmmakers can minimize downtime and maximize productivity, ultimately optimizing the efficiency of the entire production process.

One highly effective strategy is to organize scenes by location, grouping together those that take place in the same or nearby areas. This approach significantly reduces travel time between sets, allowing the crew to devote more time to capturing footage and less time on the road. As a result, shooting efficiency is enhanced, and the risk of unnecessary disruptions or delays is mitigated.

Furthermore, maintaining adaptability and agility during filming is paramount for navigating the unpredictable nature of production. Despite meticulous planning, unforeseen challenges and obstacles are bound to arise on set. Whether it's unexpected weather conditions, equipment malfunctions, or last-minute changes to the script, filmmakers must be prepared to think on their feet and make quick decisions to keep the production on track. This ability to pivot and adapt in real-time is what separates successful productions from those that falter under pressure.

By fostering a culture of flexibility and resilience among the crew, filmmakers can ensure that they make the most of available resources and overcome challenges efficiently. This agility enables swift problem-solving and empowers the team to navigate any hurdles that may arise during filming. Ultimately, it is this adaptability that allows productions to stay on schedule and achieve their objectives within the allocated timeframe, ensuring that the vision of the film is brought to life in its entirety.

7. **Post-Production**: In the realm of post-production, navigating budget constraints can be a daunting task, but with strategic approaches, filmmakers can still achieve high-quality results without overspending. One viable

strategy is to take on the editing process independently or collaborate with a talented editor who is willing to work within the project's financial limitations. This not only allows for greater control over the creative vision but also helps to minimize costs, as hiring professional editors can be a significant expense.

Moreover, leveraging free or affordable sound editing tools can be a game-changer in enhancing the overall quality of the film's sound without exceeding the budget. These tools offer a plethora of options for manipulating audio elements, from adjusting levels and adding effects to cleaning up background noise. By incorporating these tools into the post-production workflow, filmmakers can elevate the auditory experience of their film without incurring substantial costs.

Similarly, opting for cost-effective color grading techniques can significantly enhance the visual aesthetics of the film without the need for expensive software or services. From adjusting contrast and saturation to fine-tuning color balance, there are numerous ways to achieve professional-grade color grading using readily available tools and resources. By employing these techniques judiciously, filmmakers can give their film a polished and cohesive look that captivates audiences without straining the budget.

Overall, by embracing these budget-friendly approaches to post-production, filmmakers can strike a balance between creative excellence and financial prudence. Through careful planning, resourcefulness, and a willingness to explore alternative solutions, it is possible to achieve professional results that meet or even exceed expectations while staying within budgetary constraints. Ultimately, the key lies in finding innovative ways to maximize the available resources and bring the filmmaker's vision to life without compromising on quality.

By following these detailed instructions and maintaining a resourceful and creative approach, you can effectively manage an ultra-low budget film shoot and produce a quality film within financial constraints.

Moreover, effective communication and collaboration are the cornerstones of successful production management. By fostering a culture of teamwork and transparency, filmmakers empower their crew to work together toward a common goal, overcoming challenges and achieving success against all odds.

The production phase is a crucible of creativity and collaboration, where scripts are transformed into cinematic reality. By exploring the fundamentals of cinematography, offering techniques for directing actors, and discussing strategies for managing time, resources, and unexpected challenges, this chapter equips filmmakers with the knowledge and tools they need to navigate the complexities of production with confidence and creativity. With careful planning, ingenuity, and perseverance, you can harness the magic of filmmaking and bring your stories to life on screen for audiences to enjoy and cherish for generations to come.

Chapter 8: Bringing Your Vision to Life in Post-Production

After the cameras have stopped rolling and the final scene has been captured, the journey of filmmaking is far from over. Welcome to the world of post-production, where raw footage is transformed into a polished cinematic masterpiece. In Chapter 8, we delve into the intricacies of the post-production process, from editing and sound design to visual effects. We'll explore popular editing software and techniques, discuss the importance of collaboration and feedback, and highlight the iterative nature of achieving your artistic vision.

Overview of the Post-Production Process

Post-production is the stage where the magic truly happens. It is here that the disparate elements of filmmaking - the footage, sound, and visual effects - are woven together to create a cohesive and compelling narrative. The post-production process typically includes three main phases: editing, sound design, and visual effects.

Editing is the backbone of post-production, where the raw footage is transformed into a coherent story. Editors sift through hours of footage, selecting the best takes, and arranging them in a sequence that captures the essence of the script. They refine pacing, adjust timing, and fine-tune transitions to create a seamless flow from scene to scene.

Sound design adds depth and dimension to the auditory experience of the film. Sound designers layer dialogue, music, and sound effects to create a rich and immersive soundscape that enhances the emotional impact of the story. From subtle ambient noises to bombastic explosions, every sound is carefully crafted to evoke a specific mood or emotion.

Visual effects are the icing on the cake, adding a touch of magic to the world of the film. Whether creating fantastical creatures, breathtaking landscapes, or dazzling special effects, visual effects artists use cutting-edge technology to bring the director's vision to life on screen.

Popular Editing Software and Techniques

One of the most critical aspects of post-production is editing, where the raw footage is sculpted into a cohesive narrative. There are several popular editing software programs available, each with its own set of features and capabilities.

Adobe Premiere Pro is a widely used editing software that offers a comprehensive suite of tools for editing, color grading, and audio mixing. Its intuitive interface and robust feature set make it a favorite among filmmakers of all levels.

Avid Media Composer is another industry-standard editing software known for its stability and precision. With powerful editing tools and advanced media management capabilities, Avid is favored by professional editors working on complex and large-scale projects.

Final Cut Pro X is a popular choice among Mac users, offering a streamlined editing workflow and a wide range of creative tools. Its intuitive interface and seamless integration with other Apple products make it an ideal choice for filmmakers working in the Apple ecosystem.

When delving into the realm of film editing, it's essential to grasp fundamental principles that underpin the art form. Among these, pacing stands out as a cornerstone element, influencing the rhythm and tempo of the entire film. Pacing is not merely about the speed at which scenes unfold but rather the deliberate manipulation of time to evoke specific emotional responses from the audience.

Editors wield pacing as a powerful tool, orchestrating the arrangement of shots, the duration of cuts, and the use of transitions to create tension, suspense, or emotional resonance. By strategically adjusting these elements, editors can control the flow of the narrative, guiding viewers through moments of calm reflection or heart-pounding action with precision and finesse.

In addition to pacing, continuity editing plays a vital role in maintaining coherence and clarity in visual storytelling. This technique ensures that the spatial and temporal relationships between shots remain consistent throughout the film, allowing for seamless transitions between scenes. Continuity editing relies on a series of established conventions, including matching action, eye-line matches, and establishing shots, to create a sense of continuity and immersion for the audience.

By adhering to these principles, editors can avoid jarring discrepancies that might distract viewers and detract from the overall cinematic experience. Instead, they can craft a cohesive narrative that unfolds seamlessly, drawing audiences into the world of the film and keeping them engaged from beginning to end.

In essence, mastering editing techniques such as pacing and continuity editing is essential for aspiring filmmakers seeking to tell compelling stories through the medium of film. By understanding the principles behind these techniques and applying them with skill and precision, editors can elevate their work from mere assembly to artistry, creating films that resonate with audiences on a profound and emotional level.

Importance of Collaboration, Feedback, and Iteration

While editing may seem like a solitary endeavor, it is, in fact, a collaborative process that relies on input and feedback from a diverse team of creatives. Directors, producers, editors, and sound designers work together to refine the film's narrative, enhance its emotional impact, and achieve the director's artistic vision.

Collaboration is essential to the success of post-production, as it allows for the exchange of ideas, perspectives, and expertise. Directors collaborate closely with editors to articulate their vision and provide creative direction, while editors draw on their technical skills and artistic sensibilities to bring that vision to life on screen.

Feedback is another crucial aspect of the editing process, providing valuable insights and perspectives from fresh eyes. Screenings and test screenings allow filmmakers to gauge audience reactions, identify areas for improvement, and make informed decisions about pacing storytelling, and visual aesthetics.

Iteration is the key to achieving perfection in post-production. Editors continually refine their work based on feedback and experimentation, fine-tuning every detail until the film reaches its full potential. It is through this iterative process of trial and error that the magic of filmmaking truly comes to life, as the film evolves from a rough assemblage of footage to a polished and captivating cinematic experience.

Post-production is the final frontier of filmmaking, where raw footage is transformed into a polished masterpiece through the alchemy of editing, sound design, and visual effects. By providing an overview of the post-production process, introducing popular editing software and techniques, and discussing the importance of collaboration, feedback, and iteration, this chapter serves as a comprehensive guide for filmmakers as they navigate the intricacies of bringing their vision to life on screen.

With dedication, creativity, and a collaborative spirit, filmmakers can harness the power of post-production to create cinematic experiences that captivate, inspire, and endure for generations to come.

Conclusion: Embracing Your Filmmaking Journey

As you reach the culmination of your filmmaking journey, it's an opportune moment to pause and reflect on the profound impact that this art form has had on your life and creative journey. Throughout the pages of this book, we've embarked on a comprehensive exploration of the multifaceted world of filmmaking, delving into the nuances of storytelling, the complexities of production, and the transformative process of post-production. Each chapter has been a steppingstone, guiding you through the intricacies of the filmmaking process and equipping you with the knowledge and skills necessary to bring your vision to life on screen.

Now, as you stand on the threshold of a new chapter, it's imperative to internalize the lessons learned and embrace the personal growth that has unfolded throughout your filmmaking odyssey. Beyond the technical aspects of the craft, filmmaking has the remarkable ability to catalyze profound introspection and self-discovery. It challenges you to confront your strengths and weaknesses, to push the boundaries of your creativity, and to navigate the ever-evolving landscape of storytelling with courage and resilience.

As you embark on the next phase of your filmmaking journey, remember to carry with you the invaluable insights gleaned from this experience. Embrace the spirit of exploration and curiosity that has fueled your passion for storytelling thus far, and allow it to guide you toward new horizons of innovation and creativity. Whether you're refining your skills as a director, honing your craft as a cinematographer, or experimenting with new techniques in post-production, approach each endeavor with an open mind and a willingness to push the boundaries of what's possible.

Above all, remember that filmmaking is not just a technical pursuit but a deeply personal and transformative journey. It's an opportunity to channel your unique perspective and voice into a medium that has the power to inspire, provoke thought, and evoke emotion on a profound level. So as you bid farewell to this chapter and set your sights on the future, do so with the knowledge that your journey as a filmmaker is a lifelong odyssey—one filled with boundless possibilities, endless discovery, and the potential to leave an indelible mark on the world of cinema.

Reflecting on the Transformative Power of Filmmaking

For many filmmakers, the journey begins as a simple passion or curiosity, but it often evolves into a profound catalyst for personal growth and self-discovery. Through the process of bringing stories to life on screen, we confront our fears, challenge our assumptions, and uncover truths about ourselves and the world around us.

Consider the journey of Mia, a budding filmmaker who embarked on her first project with little more than a camera and a dream. Along the way, she encountered setbacks, doubts, and moments of uncertainty. Yet, with each obstacle she faced, Mia discovered newfound resilience, creativity, and determination within herself.

Through the lens of filmmaking, Mia learned to see the world with fresh eyes, to find beauty in the mundane, and to capture moments of profound meaning and emotion. She discovered the power of storytelling to connect people across boundaries of culture, language, and experience, and she found her voice as an artist, storyteller, and advocate for change.

Encouraging Continued Experimentation, Exploration, and Innovation

As you continue your filmmaking journey, remember to embrace the spirit of experimentation, exploration, and innovation. Don't be afraid to push the boundaries of your creativity, challenge conventions, and take risks in pursuit of your artistic vision.

Take inspiration from the story of Marcus, a filmmaker who refused to be bound by the constraints of traditional filmmaking. Instead of following the well-trodden path, Marcus sought out new techniques, new perspectives, and new collaborators who shared his passion for innovation and experimentation.

Through his bold approach to filmmaking, Marcus discovered new ways of storytelling, new modes of expression, and new audiences hungry for fresh and original content. He embraced emerging technologies, unconventional techniques, and non-traditional distribution channels to share his work with the world, and in doing so, he inspired a new generation of filmmakers to chart their own course and follow their own creative instincts.

Providing Resources and Next Steps

As you embark on the next phase of your filmmaking journey, remember that you are not alone. There is a vast community of filmmakers, educators, and industry professionals ready to support and guide you along the way.

Seek out resources for furthering your education, I have touched on a few of them here:

1. **Back to One eBook**: A comprehensive guide covering all aspects of filmmaking, from pre-production to post-production, including technical information, industry standards, and practical advice.

2. **Online Courses and Tutorials**: Platforms like the Stay Connected online Film Academy, Udemy, Coursera, and MasterClass offer a wide range of online courses and tutorials covering various aspects of filmmaking, from scriptwriting and cinematography to editing and sound design.

3. **Filmmaking Books**: Numerous books on filmmaking offer in-depth insights into specific areas of the craft. Some essential titles include "Save the Cat!" by Blake Snyder for screenwriting, "In the Blink of an Eye" by

Walter Murch for editing, and "Rebel Without a Crew" by Robert Rodriguez for independent filmmaking.

4. **Film Festivals and Screenings**: Attending film festivals and screenings is an excellent way to immerse yourself in the world of cinema, discover new talent, and learn from established filmmakers through Q&A sessions and panel discussions.

5. **Industry Websites and Blogs**: Websites like No Film School, IndieWire, and Filmmaker Magazine provide valuable resources, news, and insights into the latest trends and developments in the film industry. In addition, subscribe to the 2-g4me.com site for extra resources.

6. **Networking Events and Workshops**: Networking events, workshops, and meetups offer opportunities to connect with other filmmakers, industry professionals, and potential collaborators, as well as to learn from their experiences and expertise.

7. **Film Production Software**: Software tools like Adobe Premiere Pro, Final Cut Pro X, and DaVinci Resolve are essential for editing and post-production, while Celtx and StudioBinder can assist with scriptwriting, pre-production planning, and scheduling.

8. **Film School Programs**: While not essential, attending a reputable film school program can provide structured education, hands-on experience, and valuable networking opportunities that can accelerate your filmmaking career.

9. **Film Equipment Rentals**: Renting film equipment from rental houses or online platforms like ShareGrid and Lensrentals allows you to access professional-grade gear without the high upfront costs of purchasing.

10. **Film Production Communities**: Online communities such as Reddit's r/Filmmakers (https://www.reddit.com/r/Filmmakers/), filmmaking forums like DVXuser (https://www.dvxuser.com/) and Creative Cow (https://creativecow.net/), and social

media groups provide spaces for filmmakers to connect, share knowledge, seek advice, and collaborate on projects.

By utilizing these essential filmmaking resources, aspiring filmmakers can gain valuable knowledge, skills, and connections to help them succeed in the competitive world of cinema.

Whether through workshops, seminars, or online courses. Connect with fellow filmmakers through networking events, film festivals, and online forums to share ideas, collaborate on projects, and find mentorship and support.

Consider the story of Emily, a filmmaker who found her tribe in the vibrant community of independent filmmakers. Through networking events, film festivals, and online forums, Emily forged connections with like-minded creatives who shared her passion for storytelling and her commitment to pushing the boundaries of the medium.

Through collaboration and shared experience, Emily discovered new opportunities for growth, learning, and professional development. She found mentors who offered guidance and support, collaborators who challenged and inspired her, and friends who became her creative family.

In conclusion, your filmmaking journey is a testament to your passion, creativity, and resilience. As you reflect on the lessons learned, the challenges overcome, and the successes achieved, remember to embrace the transformative power of filmmaking and the personal growth it has fostered within you.

Continue to experiment, explore, and innovate in your filmmaking practice, pushing the boundaries of your creativity and challenging conventions. Seek out resources and next steps for furthering your education, networking with industry professionals, and sharing your work with the world.

With dedication, perseverance, and a commitment to lifelong learning and growth, you can harness the power of filmmaking to tell stories that inspire, provoke thought, and spark change in the world. Embrace your journey, embrace your creativity, and embrace the limitless possibilities that lie ahead.

###

www.ingramcontent.com/pod-product-compliance
Lightning Source LLC
Chambersburg PA
CBHW030442220526
45464CB00006B/2379